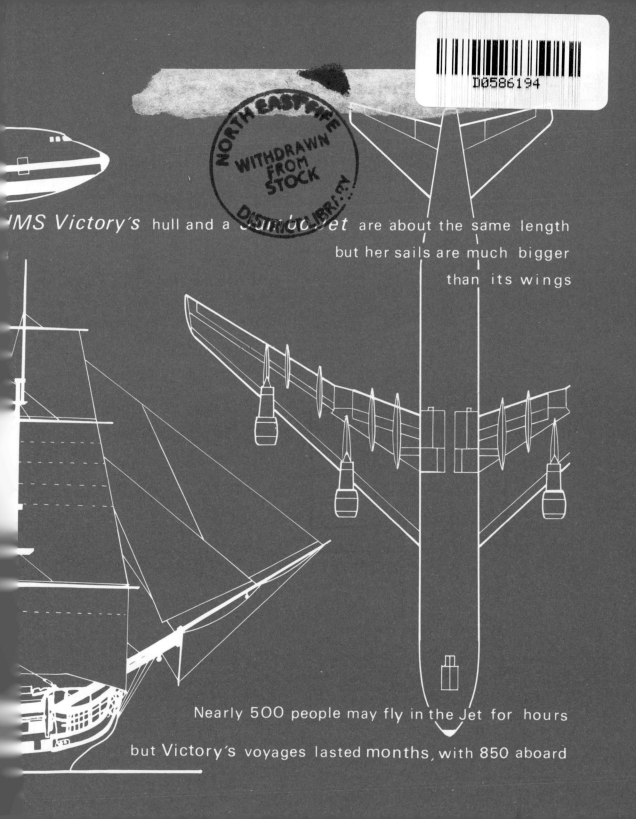

HMS Victory's hull and a Jumbo Jet are about the same length

but her sails are much bigger

than its wings

Nearly 500 people may fly in the Jet for hours

but Victory's voyages lasted months, with 850 aboard

Ian Morrison

How they lived in

a Sailing Ship
of War

13

Lutterworth Press · Guildford · Surrey · England

Nowadays, warships are moved by engines that use oil or even nuclear energy. However, right up to the nineteenth century, the only power for ships was the strength of the crew's muscles and the force of the wind.

The larger ships were far too heavy to row, and had to depend on sails. Steering them without any engines needed great skill, since winds and currents seldom went in the direction the captain wanted. The biggest sailing warships had hulls over 60 metres long by 15 metres wide (200 feet by 50 feet), and weighed over 3550 tonnes. Yet they were not made of steel, but of wood. Whole forests were felled to build them, for it took enormous amounts of timber to make them strong enough to resist stormy seas and cannon balls.

The guided missiles and torpedoes used by today's navies had not been invented. Neither had the gun turrets which can swing modern guns round to fire from either side of the ship. Instead there were cannons which were fired through rows of trapdoors in the hull, called 'gunports'. The crew had to swing the whole ship 'broadside on' to the enemy to get the cannons pointing at him, so this was called 'giving him a broadside'. Since wooden ships were difficult to sink, sea fights often went on until one crew managed to swarm aboard the enemy ship with cutlasses, to fight hand to hand.

Such battles were going on well before the time of the Spanish Armada, back in the sixteenth century, but one of the most famous of all fights between sailing warships was fought off Trafalgar in 1805, when the French Emperor, Napoleon, was trying to conquer Britain.

HMS Victory, *the winning flagship, is preserved at Portsmouth in England, where people can visit her. In America* USS Constitution, *a beautiful sailing frigate from the same period, is also open to visitors. This book tells what life was like aboard* Victory *at the time of the Battle of Trafalgar.*

In the days of the sailing Navy, boys went to sea very young. A big ship like *Victory* would have seventy or eighty boys aboard, and they often became the best sailors in the Navy when they grew up. Some boys were sent to sea whether they liked it or not, because they had been rogues at home, but others went willingly. When the Navy was short of sailors, a 'Press Gang' might be sent ashore to kidnap men from the streets and fields. But there is a Navy saying, 'A volunteer is worth ten pressed men', meaning that a keen lad is far more use than a lot of unwilling men who have been dragged aboard.

Even though he was keen to go, Jack still found it very sad to leave his family.

When he gets aboard for the first time, Jack finds the ship a
very confusing place, divided up by floors which the sailors
call 'decks' and walls which they call 'bulkheads'. To give
some idea of what *Victory* is like, part of the side is shown
here as if it is glass, so that you can see in. But the real
Victory is built of wood, and it takes Jack ages to find his
way around below decks. The darkness makes it more
difficult. Except in the big cabins in the stern (where the
Admiral and Captain work), there are no windows.
Daylight only gets in when hatchways or gunports are
opened.

Jack peers about in the flickering light from smoky candles in lanterns. The beams from which the lanterns hang are so low that the taller sailors have to move about in a stoop to keep from bashing their heads on the solid oak. Jack isn't big enough yet to have to worry about that, but in the gloom he does keep stubbing his toes on bolts, with iron rings through them, which stick up from the planking in rows. These are for ropes, to haul the cannons about. There seem to be cannons everywhere, and one of the sailors tells him that there are a hundred aboard.

The cannons are different sizes. Down on the main gundeck Jack finds great big ones that fire balls weighing 32 pounds (14½ kg). On the middle deck are 24-pounders (11 kg); on the upper decks are 12-pounders (5½ kg) plus two 68-pounder monsters (31 kg)! The guns themselves weigh tons, and Jack will clearly have to grow a lot before he can help to heave them about.

In fact, Jack can hardly shift the bigger cannon balls in their racks on the deck, let alone lift one to load it into a cannon. He is trying this when the boatswain asks him what on earth he is up to . . .

The boatswain explains that in a battle, boys like Jack act as 'powder-monkeys', bringing the gunpowder (which doesn't weigh so much) while the big sailors handle the guns. Firing the cannons takes lots of strong men, and you need even more men to sail the ship, turning her so your broadsides hit the enemy. *HMS Victory* needs 850 men in her crew.

Cannons aboard HMS Victory; *note also the mess table and benches*

Crowded with cannons – crowded with hundreds and
hundreds of sailors – *Victory* seems a noisy, tiring place.
Somebody is rolling barrels along the deck just above Jack's
head, and their booming makes the boatswain roar even
louder at his gang stowing spare sails. Even Jack's mother
never shouted at him quite that loud!

Whistles blow, and a strange order comes: 'All Hands, Pipe
Down'. Everything goes quiet: it is bed-time. Jack hasn't
seen a bed anywhere – and there surely isn't room for the
number they'd all need . . . But the sailors are bringing
hammocks, and the boatswain's mate slings one for him
too. It is really quite comfortable, after he finds out how to
stay in it . . .

7

Morning comes horribly early, but Jack tries to copy the sailors who are stowing their bedding and spare clothes in their hammocks and tying them up as neat canvas sausages. Jack's doesn't quite work, and when he rushes on deck to store it with theirs in the hammock nettings, it bursts open and spews his stockings all over the deck. Jack is afraid the boatswain will roar, but he just growls (fairly quietly) and shows him the proper knots to use. If Jack isn't quick, his bedding will be soaked by the sailors who are swabbing down the decks with sea-water, while others, on their knees, grind away the dirt with blocks of rough sandstone they call 'holystones'.

Jack decides that although the boatswain is certainly terribly tough, it is probably force of habit from shouting down gales of wind that makes him roar so. Despite his ferocious whiskers, the ship's cat likes him, and that seems a good sign. So when Jack wonders why the hammocks are stowed where spray or rain might wet them, he plucks up courage to ask. Luckily, it turns out to be a sensible question. The gundecks down below are so cramped that if the hammocks were stored there, the sailors wouldn't be able to work the cannons quickly enough if they met the enemy. Putting them in nets round the rail also gives men and boys on the upper deck protection from musket shots.

Whistles sound again, piping 'Hands to Breakfast'. The boatswain tells Jack that one of his other jobs as a powder-monkey is to fetch meals for the gunners. Because fires are so dangerous in a wooden ship, all the cooking is done in one big galley, where the boys collect food for the gun crews. This sounds easy, but the crews eat by their own cannons, and if your gun is at the other end of the ship from the galley you have to run. With ring-bolts to trip over, and ladders between decks to climb, accidents can happen, particularly if the ship is rolling about in a storm. Your large hairy messmates will not be interested in excuses if their dinner arrives cold or ends up swilling in the bilges where stinking water gathers in the bottom of the hull . . .

Each 'mess' of seamen feeds at a table set between the cannons. The table and their benches are stowed away at the end of the meal, to free the guns. The powder-monkey sits on the biscuit barrel at the end of the table.

Ship's biscuits are baked very hard and dry since they have to keep for months (sometimes even years). The sailors get fed up with them, but beetles called 'weevils' love them. Jack soon learns to tap his biscuit sharply on the table to warn the weevils to jump out before he sinks his teeth in.

Sea-breezes give a good appetite, and with the heavy work of climbing masts, handling sails, hauling ropes and heaving cannons about, the men and boys of *Victory* are a hungry lot. Since there are 850 of them, and since *Victory* is often at sea for months on end, space has to be found for storing vast quantities of food and drinking water. The upper decks must be kept clear for working the cannons, so the stores are packed into holds below the waterline. Most of the spare cannon balls are kept there too, because they are so heavy, though there are always some in racks next to the guns, kept handy in case of surprise attacks.

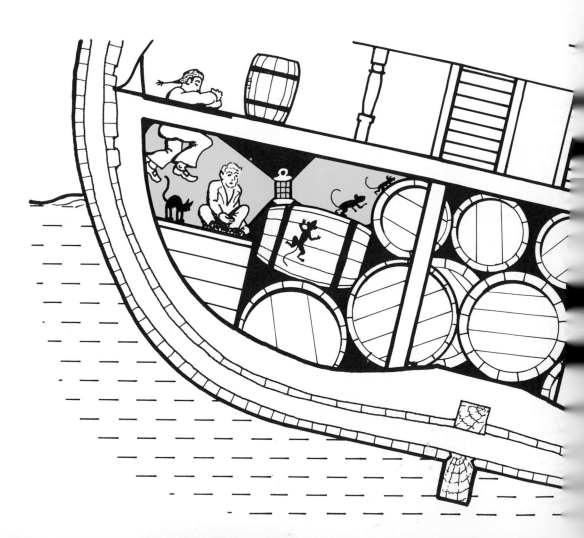

Down in the hold it is dark, and fairly nasty. The biscuit room is all right (if you don't think about all those busy weevils): at least it is dry. But the hold is damp. All wooden ships leak a little, gathering dirty water in the bilges. Jack has been sent to help bring up a barrel of pickled pork for the crew's dinner. He has to crawl over slimy casks of drinking water. Rats skitter away from the lantern light. Timbers groan as the ship heaves, and the bilge-water sloshes and stinks. Suddenly he doesn't feel much like dinner . . . He is just a *little* seasick, and soon feels fine again when he gets back to the fresh air.

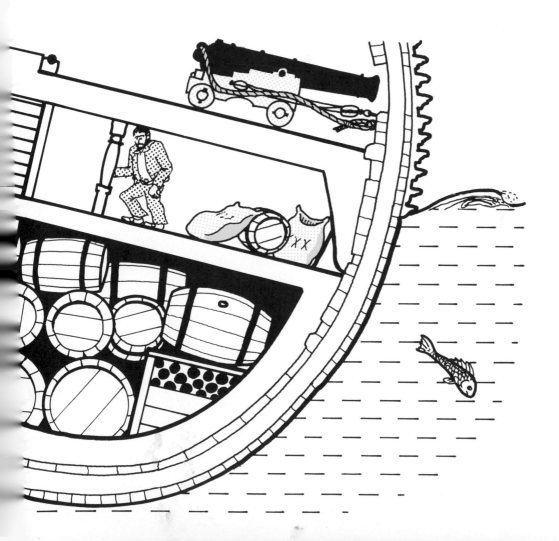

Keeping all those crowded sailors healthy was a big problem in the sailing Navy. More men died from disease and from accidents (such as falling from the masts) than were ever killed in battle.

Sometimes whole crews were almost wiped out if an infectious disease like yellow fever got aboard. Even when there was no infection, it was hard to live on nothing but dry biscuits and ancient salted beef or pork for months on end. The sailors' hair and teeth fell out and their gums went black and spongy. This was called 'scurvy'. One way of preventing it, if you couldn't get other fruit or fresh vegetables, was to make everybody drink a little lime juice every day. A lime tastes bitter, like a lemon, and American sailors were amused at the Royal Navy men being made to 'take their medicine': they still sometimes call Englishmen 'limeys', though they've mostly forgotten why.

Almost all the fresh water that could be carried was needed for cooking and drinking – even though it sometimes became horrible during a long voyage. Little could be spared for washing, so sea-water had to be used.

Ashore, very few houses had proper flushing lavatories, and there were none aboard ship. The sailors went to 'the Heads'. There, right in the front of the ship, in the bows, Jack discovered wooden seats perched over dark holes, directly above the cold waves of the ocean far below. It was clean, but very draughty.

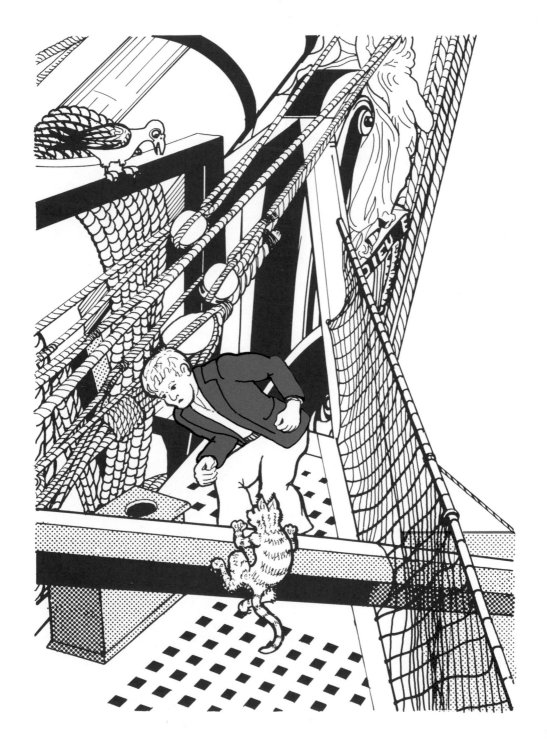

After Jack comes back from the Heads, it is soon time for lessons. The midshipmen are being taught navigation. One day they will be officers, and will have to guide their ships across the oceans, far out of sight of land. They are learning how to measure the height of the sun at midday, and then, by complicated sums, to work out the ship's position. Some of them are not very good at it yet, and the navigating officer gets very annoyed with them when they make mistakes (especially with the boy whose sum seems to put *Victory* on top of a Welsh mountain, instead of in the harbour at Portsmouth). Jack is glad he isn't a midshipman.

Jack and the other powder-monkeys learn from the
boatswain about splicing ropes and tying knots. Aboard
ship, as well as holding tight, knots must be easy to undo.
Splicing amazes Jack. He had not realised that you can take
the ends of ropes, unwind their strands, and then join them
strongly by weaving them together again. The boatswain
explains that it is important to be able to do this quickly. If
the enemy's cannon balls break the ropes which control
Victory's sails, fast repairs are necessary. Sometimes enemy
ships fire double cannon balls, each pair joined by a length
of chain, which whirl through the air and slash the ropes.

There were certainly plenty of ropes aboard *Victory* for the enemy to aim at. (Some, but by no means all, are shown in the pictures in this book.) It took literally kilometres of rope to make *Victory* work.

A sailing ship's mainmast might be a metre or more thick, but the pressure of the wind on the sails (and the heaving of the hull in the waves) would soon have snapped it off, if it had not been steadied by heavy ropes. These ropes were called the 'standing' rigging, because they 'stood', being fixed tight so that they would not move.

The sails hung from 'yards' of wood, slung across the masts. More ropes were needed to raise and lower these yards and swing them round (controlling their angles to the wind, so that the ship could change direction). These moveable ropes 'ran' through pulley blocks and were called 'running' rigging. So were the ropes which were fixed to the sails themselves, for adjusting their shape to catch the wind, and to reduce sail if the wind got too strong.

Other ropes were used to hoist the ship's rowing boats aboard or to lower them into the sea; to shift cargo, like barrels of beef; and again, more simply, for the crew to hang on to as they climbed the rigging.

Depending on the jobs they had to do, some of these ropes were cords as thin as your finger, while others were cables as thick as your thigh – or even your whole body.

The biggest ropes of all were the anchor cables – great hairy monsters, 70 centimetres round (28 inches). They had to be strong to cope with the tugs and jerks given by 3550 tonnes of ship.

Imagine a stormy night with a strong current dragging at the huge hull. Great waves beat at the bows. The wind pushes at the tall wooden sides. Even with all the sails furled, the gale grasps at the towering masts and yards, and howls through those kilometres of rope spread across the sky. Down below in the briny gloom, the anchors dig into the sea bed. So as not to be dragged away or broken, they must be big and strong. *Victory's* anchors are over six metres long (20 feet) and are made of iron and oak.

The massive anchor of HMS Victory *in dry dock, Portsmouth Harbour*

To Jack's surprise, the powder-monkeys have a special part to play in bringing up the anchor. He had thought it would all be done by the biggest sailors, but boys are needed exactly because they are little and can scoot between bigger folk's legs. The sailors use the capstan to heave in the anchor, all stamping round, thrusting at its bars. But the anchor cable is so thick and stiff that they cannot wind it round the capstan drum. A thinner rope, the 'messenger', runs in a long loop from the bows to the capstan, then back again, creeping along the deck alongside the anchor cable as the men push round and round.

Fixed to the messenger are short tails of strong rope. Jack has to seize a tail and wrap it round the great anchor cable, 'nipping' it to the loop so that as the capstan turns, the messenger drags the cable. Then as he gets near the capstan Jack must undo the tail he has been holding, so that the cable can be stowed away below while he dashes back to the start of the line. As both ropes are moving, he has to be very quick. Suddenly he understands why the boatswain tells him to be 'nippy' when he wants something done fast, and why he calls the boys 'little nippers'.

A fiddler plays a shanty while the men bring up the anchor. Jack soon finds that the sailors sing shanties with different rhythms to match the different jobs they do. The next job is to set sail.

To shift such a big ship without engine power needs an enormous area of sail. The sails must thrust the great hull through rough seas, with all its load of cannons, stores and people, using just the force of the wind.

When the wind is weak, all the sails are needed, but less are set if it is stronger. The sailors work along the yards, standing on foot-ropes and hanging on with their elbows, using one hand to work the ship and one to look after themselves. They tell Jack that it isn't frightening once you get used to it, but he isn't sure that he believes them. The mainmast is over 60 metres high (200 feet) and sways about all over the sky as *Victory* rolls.

The boatswain tells Jack he need only climb up halfway for his first day, but he must do it the proper sailor's way, which means hanging upside-down to get over on to the platform called the 'main top'. There is a hole in the main top, called the 'lubber's hole'; but Jack is warned that if he tries to sneak through there instead of going the 'seaman's way' even the ship's cat will laugh at him . . .

Jack has one bad moment, but the cat comes for company, and he finds it was worse thinking about the height than actually being up there. After a week he happily races the other nippers right to the very top.

At the time Jack joins *Victory*, Britain is at war with
France. Led by their remarkable Emperor, Napoleon
Bonaparte, the French have conquered much of Europe,
and forced other countries to become their allies. Jack's
first long voyage takes him right across the Atlantic, chasing
the French fleet. First the British ships sail south, past the
enemy coasts of France and Spain, to Gibraltar – the rock
fortress ruled by Britain at the mouth of the Mediterranean
Sea. Jack thinks they may sail into the Mediterranean (his
Admiral, Lord Nelson, won a great battle there some years
ago, off the mouth of the River Nile): but news comes that
the enemy ships have headed west, for America, so
Nelson's fleet chases them all the way to the Caribbean Sea.
There *Victory* searches among the West Indian islands.

At one of the islands, Trinidad, Jack goes ashore to help fill water barrels and load fresh fruit. He stares at his first palm trees and swaps his best shirt for a brightly coloured parrot that can swear in three languages. The ship's cat is not amused.

The French admiral, Villeneuve, hears that the British are on his trail. He gives them the slip among the islands and heads back for Europe again. As soon as Admiral Nelson realises that the enemy have left the Caribbean, he takes his fleet racing back across the Atlantic under full sail; but the enemy ships have too much of a lead and they get safely into port in Spain.

Only the English Channel and the British Navy stopped
Napoleon's army from invading Britain. The French fleet
waited for their chance to seize the Channel, but for much
of the war the British Navy managed to keep them
blockaded in the enemy harbours. As America's Admiral
Mahan put it, those far-distant, storm-beaten ships stood
between Napoleon and the domination of the world.
Aboard them, there could be no room for arguments, so the
sailors had to obey orders without question or face fierce
punishments. The British ships had to be there in all
weathers, risking shipwreck, prowling the sea through
gales, snow and fog, lacking shelter and fresh food for
months on end. It was an extraordinarily hard life aboard
for boys like Jack, and those who survived grew up very
tough indeed.

Horatio Nelson as a young officer leading his men

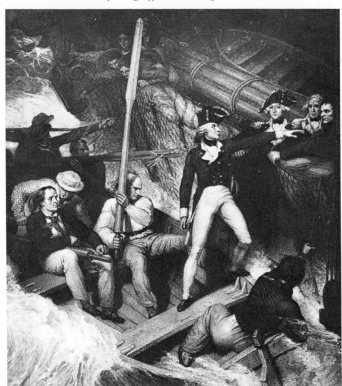

If Britain is to be safe, the enemy fleet must be lured out
and beaten once and for all. That is Lord Nelson's job. In
1805, soon after the Atlantic chase, he succeeds off Cape
Trafalgar, near Gibraltar.

At last the enemy fleet is in sight. *Victory's* Royal Marine
drummers 'beat to quarters'. This tells the sailors to rush to
their places and get the ship ready to fight. They have often
practised this, but today it feels quite different with row
after row of enemy ships sweeping up over the horizon with
their guns loaded. Quickly the sailors 'clear for action'.
They take down the bulkheads which divide up the
gundecks, and throw overboard chicken coops and anything
else that gets in the way. They light battle-lanterns and
matches for firing the guns, and then for safety put out the
galley stove. Down below the surgeon gets out his
instruments. The boatswain's men make ready to put out
any fires, splice cut rigging, and plug any leaks made by
enemy cannon balls. Now *Victory's* cannons are unlashed.

As a powder-monkey, Jack's job is to keep his mess-mates'
gun supplied with cartridges. To store gunpowder close to
the cannons would be dangerous. Instead, the casks are
kept in store-rooms called 'magazines', safe below the
waterline. Here hundreds of cloth cartridges for the
different sizes of cannons are filled ready for the battle. The
men in the magazine work by the light of a lantern shining
from behind a fire-proof window, and they wear felt slippers
instead of nailed boots, to prevent sparks. The men pass the
cartridges to the waiting powder-monkeys, who then
scamper off up the ladders and through the gundecks to
their own cannons.

At first Jack was scared that if he dropped a cartridge it
would explode, but the gunners have told him that won't
happen. Much more dangerous is the chance of getting
knocked down and flattened by a cannon, because each
time the guns are fired the explosion sends them crashing
back to the end of their ropes. When all the guns are to be
fired broadside, you can listen for the officer's order and
leap out of the way. But when the cannons are being fired
just as fast as individual guncrews can re-load them,
crashing without warning across the gloomy gundecks full of
powder-smoke, it is very dangerous for the running boys –
even without enemy cannon balls that smash into *Victory's*
hull, sending jagged splinters whirling from her timbers.

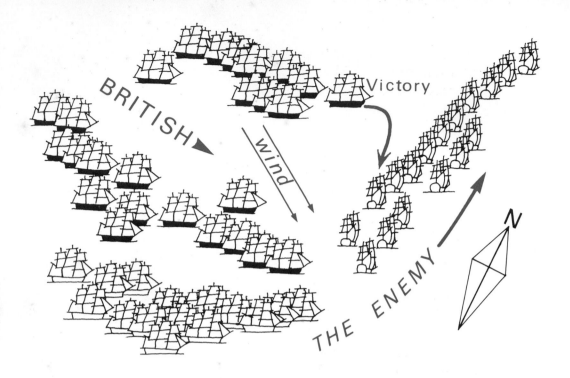

Around noon on October 21st 1805, the British and enemy fleets come together, with *Victory* leading one of the two British columns that cut into the long line of French and Spanish ships. Many men are killed by cannon fire or by musket shots from marksmen high in the rigging. One of these hits Nelson, and the wounded Admiral is carried below to the surgeon. The Frenchmen from the enemy ship *Redoutable* nearly manage to storm aboard *Victory*, but the boarders are forced back.

Lord Nelson dies, but not before he hears that the battle is won. The speed of the Royal Navy gunfire has been important to their success.

Nelson's signatures: (left) when he was a young lieutenant in 1777; (right) as Duke of Brontë in later life, one-armed and blind in one eye from wounds

Horatio Nelson   *Nelson & Bronte*

The bravery of the young powder-monkeys has had quite a bit to do with the victory. Jack has been kept so busy running between the magazine and his gun that he doesn't realise until afterwards that he must have been quite brave too.

Victory is home at last. Jack's father is proud that his son was at Trafalgar, but his mother is just relieved that he has not been hurt. She cries a bit at first, but becomes quite her old self when she suddenly notices that he has fixed his hair in a little pigtail and tarred it. He explains that this stops it blowing about when he is climbing the rigging. He thinks it makes him look every inch a sailor, but she is not impressed and utters sounds that remind him a bit of the boatswain.

Like the cat, she doesn't think much of some of the things his parrot says either – but she softens when she hears he is due to sail away again soon.

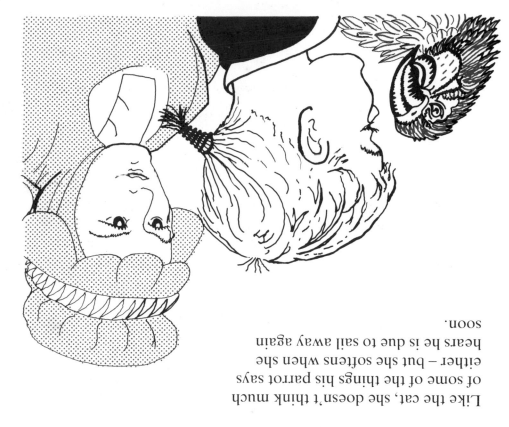

Photoset in Great Britain by
Nene Photypesetters Ltd, Northampton

Printed in Hong Kong by
Colorcraft Ltd.

PHOTOGRAPHS   The photographs on pages 6 and 19 are used by courtesy of the Royal Naval Museum, Portsmouth, to which the author and publishers express their gratitude. They also thank Mr and Mrs R. C. Barton, from whose copy of Southey's *Life of Nelson* the illustrations on pages 26 and 30 are taken.

INDEX

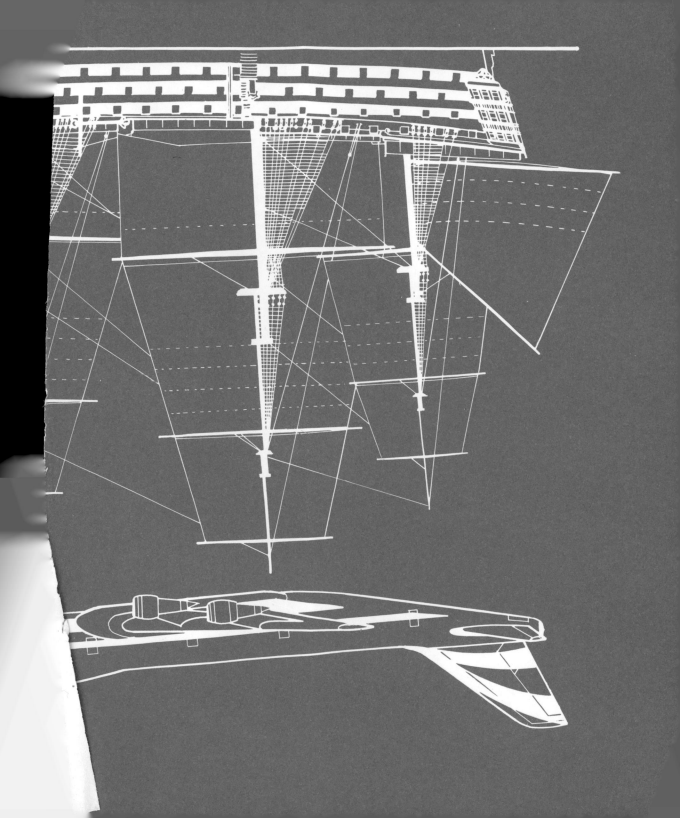